Lucy's
Kids and Money

Credit

By Lucille Tyler Baldwin
Author of the
Financially Fabulous Divas series

The day will come when our children will move out of our homes and be required to make financial decisions for themselves, such as buying or renting a place to live, buying a car, purchasing life and property insurance, starting and taking care of a family,
and more.

The pressing question that we must ask ourselves is, "Have we prepared them for the real world?"

Ann Landers said it best...

"It is not what you do for your children, but what you have prepared them to do for themselves, that will make them successful human beings."

What is Credit?

Credit is the ability of a person to secure funding to start a business, purchase a car, or to buy a house. Credit also allows you to get **goods** like a new bike, or to have a repair service done on your car before payment is due.

The bank pays for the goods or services based on the trust that repayment will be made in the future.

The 4 Most Common Types of Credit are:

1. **Revolving Credit.** This form of credit has a set amount you can spend. A credit card is an example of revolving credit.
2. **Charge Card.** A charge card balance *unlike* a credit card balance must be paid in full each month.
3. **Installment Credit.** Installment credit is repaid over time with a set number of payments. A five- year (60 payments) auto loan is an example of installment credit.
4. **Non-Installment Credit.** An example of a non-installment credit loan is a short 30-day loan. The loan is due in one lump-sum.

Adults must prove they are worthy of credit.

Adults get a
report card. It is called a
credit report.

A credit report shows banks how
adults use and repay borrowed
money.

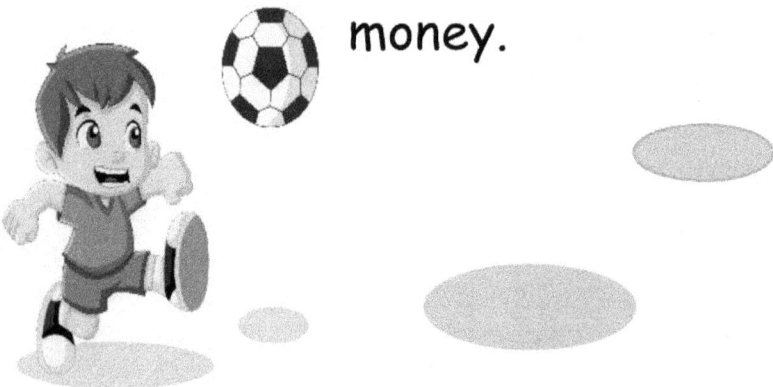

Adults do not receive letter grades such as...

A B or C

instead, adults receive a

Credit Score

also known as a

FICO SCORE.

What is a FICO SCORE?

A **FICO Score** is the most popular credit score used and it stands for:

The Fair Isaac Company.

The Fair Isaac Company is the company that created, and computes credit scores.

I will peruse your credit report.

A consumer's creditworthiness is determined by the way they manage their borrowed money.

There are three main credit-reporting bureaus/companies that give out scores:

- **TransUnion**
- **Experian**
- **Equifax**

Financial Credit Report

Different factors determine your credit score.

The 5 most important factors that determine your credit score are:

1. **Payment history: 35%**
   (do you pay your bills on time)
2. **The amount you owe: 30%**
3. **Length of credit history: 15%**
   (how long an account has been reported opened)
4. **New credit inquiries: 10%**
   (applying for new loans or credit cards)
5. **Types of credit: 10%**
   - A mortgage/buying a house
   - Car note/buying a car
   - Student loans/repaying college loans
   - Credit card debt or money loans.

Why is a Credit or FICO score so important?

CREDIT

When you borrow money, your credit score gives lenders an idea of how likely you are to repay the debt/loan.

It is important to have a good credit score because...

your credit score is used for many things such as:

- Buying a home.
- Renting a place to live.
- Buying a car.
- Car insurance.
- Electricity and water.
- Getting a cell phone.
- Starting a business (business loan).
- Applying for a job.

A good credit or FICO score is 740 or higher. A higher score tends to represent someone who is thought to make good decisions with their money.

A not so good credit score is a score that is under 600.

Your credit score determines how much **interest**, or extra money you will pay for borrowing money.

What is interest?

When you borrow money from a lender/bank you are charged a fee called **interest**.

Interest is the penalty for using someone else's money.

The higher your credit score
the less money you should pay in
interest
(unless you fall prey to a loan shark)!

Why?

Because...
lenders believe that
borrowers with a higher score
are more likely to repay the loan.

You are considered a **bad risk** if you have a low credit score. The lower your credit score the more you will pay in interest.

Why?

Lenders worry that borrowers with a lower score may not repay the loan.

What Do Lender's Want?

That is easy.

- "I want the initial loan amount (**the principal**) repaid."

- "I also want to earn a profit for lending money which is the **interest**."

What are lenders looking for when they go over a credit/loan application?

"What I have learned from experience is that the people most likely to repay a loan are those who can prove they do not need to borrow money!"

Hmm. That seems silly.

- Yes, it does seem silly, but these are people who **own** more than they are trying to borrow. They have land or other property that could be sold to repay the loan.

For example:
- If they own a house, car, or other assets that the bank could sell to recoup their money; they may be worthy of credit in the eyes of a lender.

These items are known as

collateral.

- If you do not own anything that could be used as collateral, the lender will check your **work history**.

- The lender wants to know if you **earn an income** and are in the habit of repaying your debts.

I suppose that makes sense.

- If you do not own anything of financial value that could be sold or you do not earn enough money to qualify for a loan, you may need a **cosigner**.

A cosigner is someone with good credit who is willing to be responsible for the loan.

You should spend within your means. Do not spend $100 if you only have $50.

That is silly. How can you spend $100 if you only have $50?

If you only have $50 and you borrow $50 from a friend, mom, dad, sister, or brother to buy a new $100 video game...

you are spending more money than you have available. When you borrow money, you are creating **debt**.

My DREAM CAR!

What is the big deal! I can afford the payments.

I can have anything I want. I will just use my credit cards or get a loan. That is the purpose of credit!

DEBT: The Payment Trap

If she buys the car for $10,000 with **simple interest** she could pay as much as $17,000 for her dream car!

The payment trap is believing you can afford anything you want if you can afford the monthly payments.

Remember that borrowed money **is not** your money and it comes at a cost; and that cost is interest.

Credit.

A LIFETIME of CREDIT:
up to $600,000 in interest!

4 Types of Interest

- **Simple Interest**: simple interest is charged on the principal.
- **Compound Interest**: compound interest is charged on the principal and on the interest.
- **Fixed Interest**: fixed interest the payment amount stays the same over the life of the loan.
- **Variable Interest**: variable interest rates can change weekly or monthly, and payments can increase or decrease.

Think of borrowing money as digging a hole. The more money you borrow the deeper the hole.

If you dig the hole too deep you may have a hard time repaying the borrowed money and getting out of the hole.

Repaying borrowed money means that the next time that you earn or receive money it belongs to someone else.

debt

debt

debt

debt

Why?

Because you promised to use your *future* earnings to repay **personal debt.**

Personal debt is a financial obligation that is owed for things such as clothes, cars, cell phones and loans. Personal debt is also known as **consumer debt.**

America's Consumer Debt is over 18 TRILLION DOLLARS!

$18,000,000,000,000

Wow! That is a lot of zeros!

The Path to Good Credit:

Some potential employers may check your credit score.

- Pay your bills on time.
- Keep your debt-to-income ratio low.
- Do not exceed 30% of your credit limit (credit cards or loans).
- Do not apply for a lot of credit cards and loans.
- Seek financial information.

Personal Finance Club

So, remember that learning about money is especially important and can help you make good choices with your money.

We must plan for our future.

I want to become an entrepreneur.

You should charge everything you want and pay later. You can have all that your heart desires, cars, clothes, vacations, dining out, cell phones, etc.

Does that seem like a good idea to you?

Hmm. No, that does not seem like a good idea to me.

Hmm! It seems to me that planning and saving for the future makes more sense than depending on loans and credit cards.

I agree.

Saving for Tomorrow:
TODAY

Kids Day

OPEN

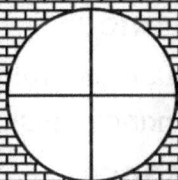

Bye for now. It is time to start planning for my future.

Glossary

Acquire
Buy or obtain.

Assets
Anything of value that can be converted into cash.

Consumer debt
The amount owed by consumers.

Goods
Items such as food, clothing, furniture, or toys.

Entrepreneur
A person who operates a business taking on greater than normal financial risks.

Loan shark
A moneylender who charges extremely high rates of interest.

Personal debt
A financial obligation that is owed by an individual or a household.

Peruse
To read through with care.

Secure
Safe, protected.

Utilization
Different types of credit such as credit cards, auto loans, student loans, or other debt.

Lucy's Kids and Money
the book series includes:

Lucy's Kids and Money: Basic Taxes

Lucy's Kids and Money: Credit

Lucy's Kids and Money: Credit Cards

Lucy's Kids and Money: Financial Mumbo Jumbo

Lucy's Kids and Money: Saving

Lucy's Kids and Money: When I Grow Up

46

Credit

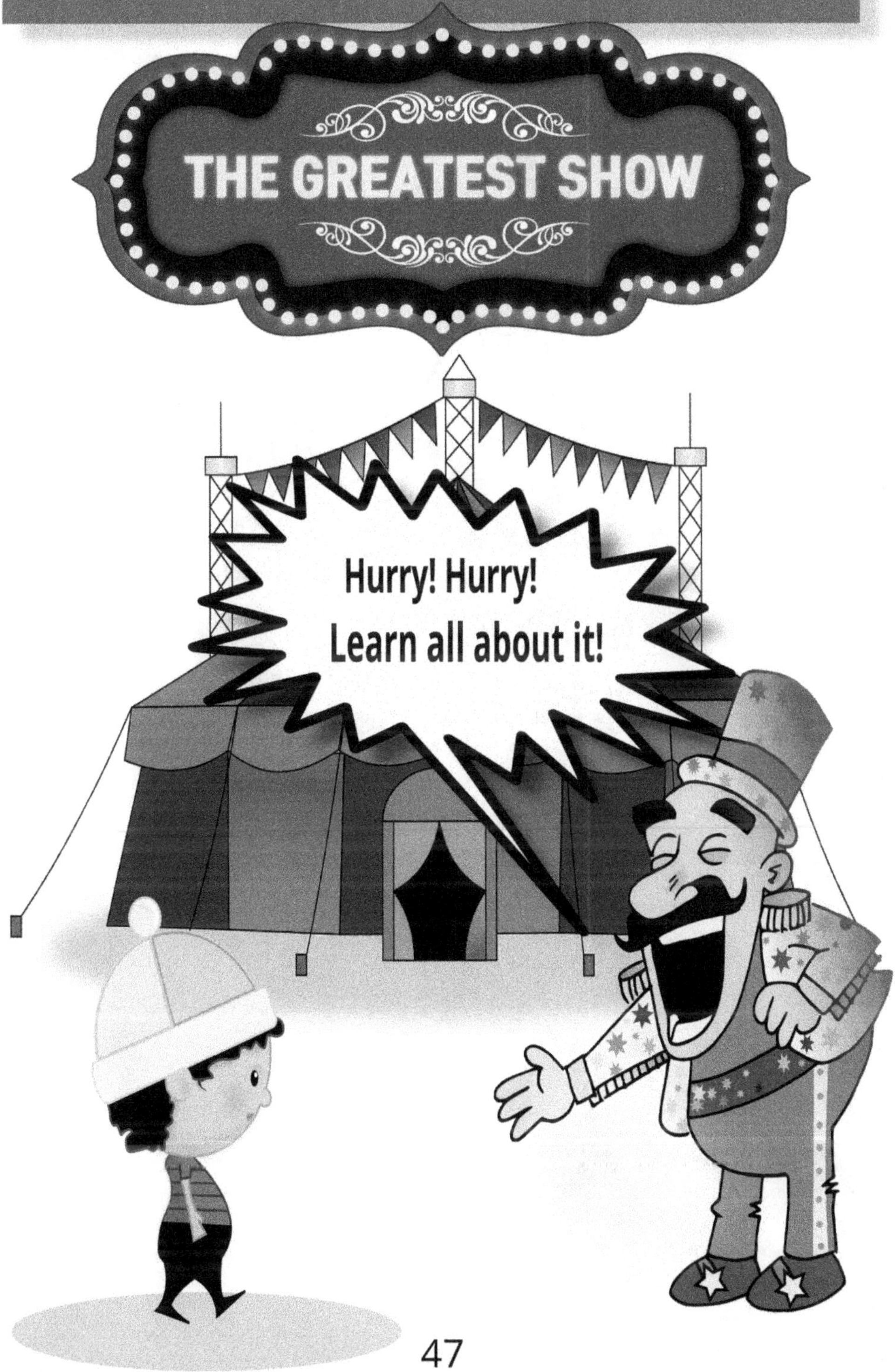

What is credit?

49

A loan is the sum of money that you borrow.

When you borrow money, you create debt.

Remember, when you borrow money you promise to repay it.

What is debt?

Debt is the amount of money you owe until you repay it.

DEBT

Do you need money? Get your loan here!

debt

That is a
great question!

Why do people borrow money?

Hmm.

People borrow money for lots of reasons.

Car Repair

Buying a car.
Appliances.
Home repairs.
Medical expenses.
Furniture.

Hello!

Cash?

Credit!

Some people borrow money to impress other people.

A Lack of Savings!

They want it NOW!

Spending without a plan!

Word Scramble

1. ROWBRO _____ Borrow

2. MNOCRESU _____

3. PYRAE _____

4. DBET _____

5. WNTSA _____

6. ENESD _____

7. GAOLS _____

8. IGDPNNSE _____

9. IVANSG _____

10. EUDTGB _____

Word Bank

**Borrow Consumer Repay
Debt Wants Needs Goals
Spending Saving Budget**

Word Search

C	R	E	D	I	T	E	D	Z	X
W	C	A	S	H	I	Z	E	E	H
B	A	N	K	Q	P	N	B	X	B
D	X	S	B	G	S	B	T	X	S
N	L	Q	U	U	L	D	L	I	P
Y	P	I	D	U	U	E	O	K	E
S	R	D	G	W	A	A	A	C	N
Q	I	X	E	T	W	R	N	O	D
Y	C	P	T	M	O	N	E	Y	B
C	E	S	A	V	E	J	X	X	I

Debt	Loan	Budget	Price
Earn	Save	Spend	Cash
Credit	Bank	Money	

True or False

Debt
is money that you owe.

61

Word Scramble

1. AKNB _____

2. CTDERI _____

3. BETD _____

4. EEINRTST _____

5. NLAO _____

6. OYNEM _____

7. OWE _____

8. AYPETNM _____

Word Bank

BANK CREDIT DEBT INTEREST
LOAN MONEY OWE PAYMENT

Consumer Debt

The amount of money owed by consumers.

The payment trap!

Repay

Debt (Owe)

Borrow Money

What is a consumer?

A consumer is a person who buys goods or services for personal needs.

I bought something just for me!

Goods -VS- Services

Goods are things you can touch. Goods are **tangible.**

Examples of Goods:
Pencils
Toys
Hamburgers
Books

I am going to buy this book.

I am buying food to cook for dinner.

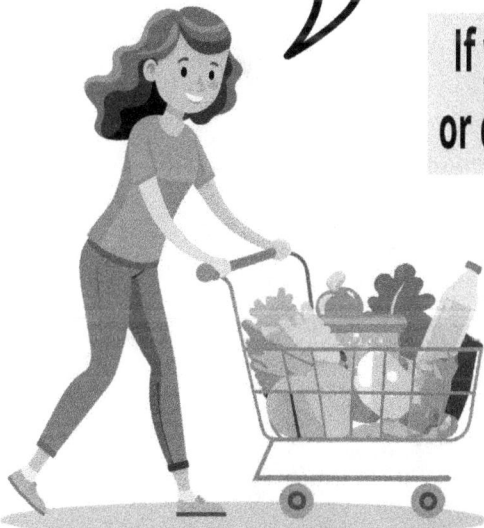

If you can pick it up, touch it, or carry it - it is a tangible item.

Examples of Services:

A service is **Intangible.**
Intangible means you cannot touch it, or hold it in your hands.

A service is something that someone does for you.

If you hire me to paint your house that is a service.

True or False

(Circle your answer)

Taking your food order is a service.

Cheeseburger, please.

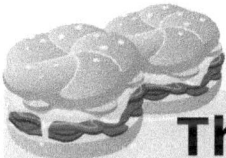

The food is a good.
You can hold the cheeseburger in your hands.

Saving money can help you use less credit.

Did You Know?

The earlier you start saving, the less likely you are to need to borrow money.

70

Joke

Why did you eat your homework?

Because the teacher said homework will be a piece of cake!

Oh brother!

True or False

(Circle your answer)

Money is what people use to buy things.

Pop Quiz

What is credit?

Circle your answer.

A.) The ability to borrow money.

B.) Money you save.

C.) Money you find on the ground.

Coloring Break

CIRCUS

Why did the dog sit in the shade?

Because he doesn't want to be a **hot** dog!

THE GREATEST SHOW

Color the Clown

Word Search
Types of Loans

```
C L U S T U D E N T
C R E D I T C A R D
T P E R S O N A L B
W A O Z A S T Q M U
K F H F Y Q O Y O S
E D U C A T I O N I
M O R T G A G E E N
U N H B S K Z L Y E
D K E V N G B A N S
C A R C E K W E D S
```

MONEY	EDUCATION	CREDIT CARD
MORTGAGE	CAR	BUSINESS
PERSONAL	STUDENT	

77

CIRCUS

Sometimes people borrow money when they want something now... but they do not have enough money yet.

True!

True or False

(Circle your answer)

Credit is...

money you borrow to buy things now, but it must be paid back later.

True

Coloring Break

Pony Ride

What is a loan?

A loan is borrowed money with a repayment plan.

Short-term goals

A short-term goal may take less than an hour, or a few weeks.

My short-term goals are to study for my spelling test next week, make up my bed, and play my video game.

Short-term goals do not take long.

Medium-term goals

Medium-term goals can take a few weeks, or months.

If I save my extra money for 2 months, I can buy a new laptop.

Long-term goals

Long-term goals can take from months to years.

Buy a Car

Save and invest for retirement

Education

Wedding/Honeymoon

Buying or Renting a house.

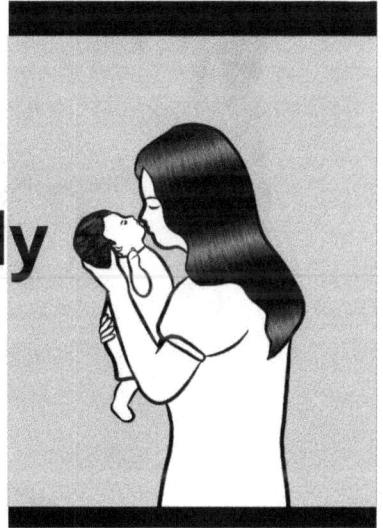

Family

Vacation

CIRCUS
Finance Meeting

How many words
can you make using the letters in

Friendship

Word Bank ➡

Debt

Afford

Credit

Repay

Income

Lender

Interest

Crossword Puzzle

Across

4. Money received from working.

5. This allows you to borrow money to buy something now and repay it later.

6. When you have enough money to pay.

7. The cost of borrowing money.

Down

1. When you return borrowed money.

2. A person that allows you to borrow money with the expectation of being repaid.

3. When you owe borrowed money.

What do you call a bear with no teeth?

When you borrow money you also pay interest.

What is interest?

Interest

Interest is a fee for using someone else's money.

The lender makes money.

Wow! You repay the money plus extra money.

If you lend your friend $10 to buy a book, and you say, "You can pay me back $11 next week." **That extra $1 is interest.**

The longer it takes you to repay the loan, the more you will pay in interest.

What does Living <u>Below</u>, <u>At</u>, or <u>Above</u> Your Means mean?

Below

If you get $10 a week and only spend $6 you are living below your means.

At

If you get $10 a week and spend $10 you are living at your means.

Above

If you get $10 a week and spend $15 you are living above your means.

How can you spend $15 if you only have $10?

Credit!

Did You Know...

that money isn't actually made out of paper?

That's right!

Wait! What?

In America dollar bills (money) are made out of a blend of 75% cotton and 25% linen.

Cotton and linen bills can last a lot longer than paper bills.

It also helps me avoid damage when I get wet!

Coloring Break

Types of Debt

Personal loans

Credit card debt

Mortgages

Students loans

Auto loans

Business loans

Medical bills

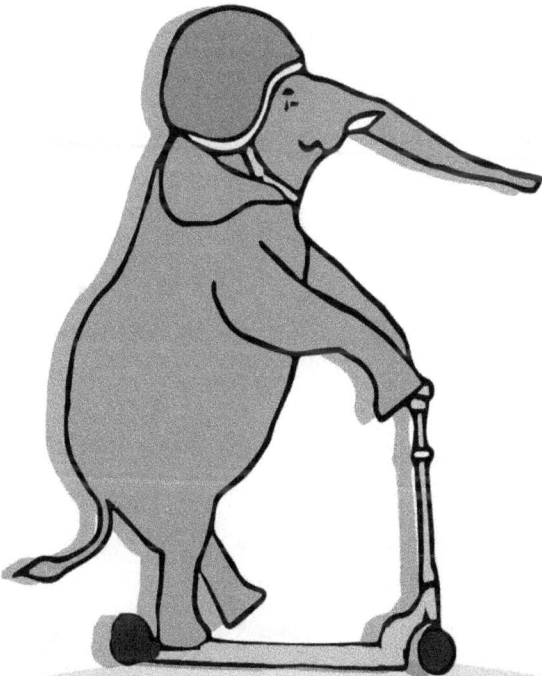

Remember...

Debt is money that you borrow with the understanding that you will repay the money in the future.

Got it.

Funny or Not Funny?

What is a great way to double your money?

Fold it in half.

What is a budget?

A budget keeps track of how much income or money you have coming in, and how you will spend, save or invest your money.

My budget is $30.00!
I received $5.00 for my allowance,
$5.00 for doing chores,
and $20.00 for my birthday.

My Budget

Income:

$ 5.00 Allowance.

$ 5.00 Chores.

$20.00 Birthday gift.

Money Outgoing:

$5.00 Savings account.

$3..00 Donate.

$5.00 Save for car.

$2.00 Repay loan from my brother.

$5.00 Save for education.

$10..00 Spend.

Creating a budget can help you manage your money.

Don't forget...

saving money can help you use less credit!

Saving money teaches you to think ahead, and make healthy money choices.

Coloring Break

1). **Short** -term

2). -term

3). -term

What are the 3 types of financial goals you can set?

Do Not Forget...

When you buy something you need or want, such as toys, clothes or video games, you become a <u>consumer</u>!

When you use borrowed money to buy these things you are creating consumer debt.

Why are goals important?

Goals help me stay focused.

Encourages a Growth Mindset!

Builds confidence!

Problem solving!

I don't need to borrow every time I want something. I can save and plan for my future.

And you can too.

www.ingramcontent.com/pod-product-compliance
Lightning Source LLC
Chambersburg PA
CBHW060818050426
42449CB00008B/1721